Variations of Love

Anthony G. Martinez

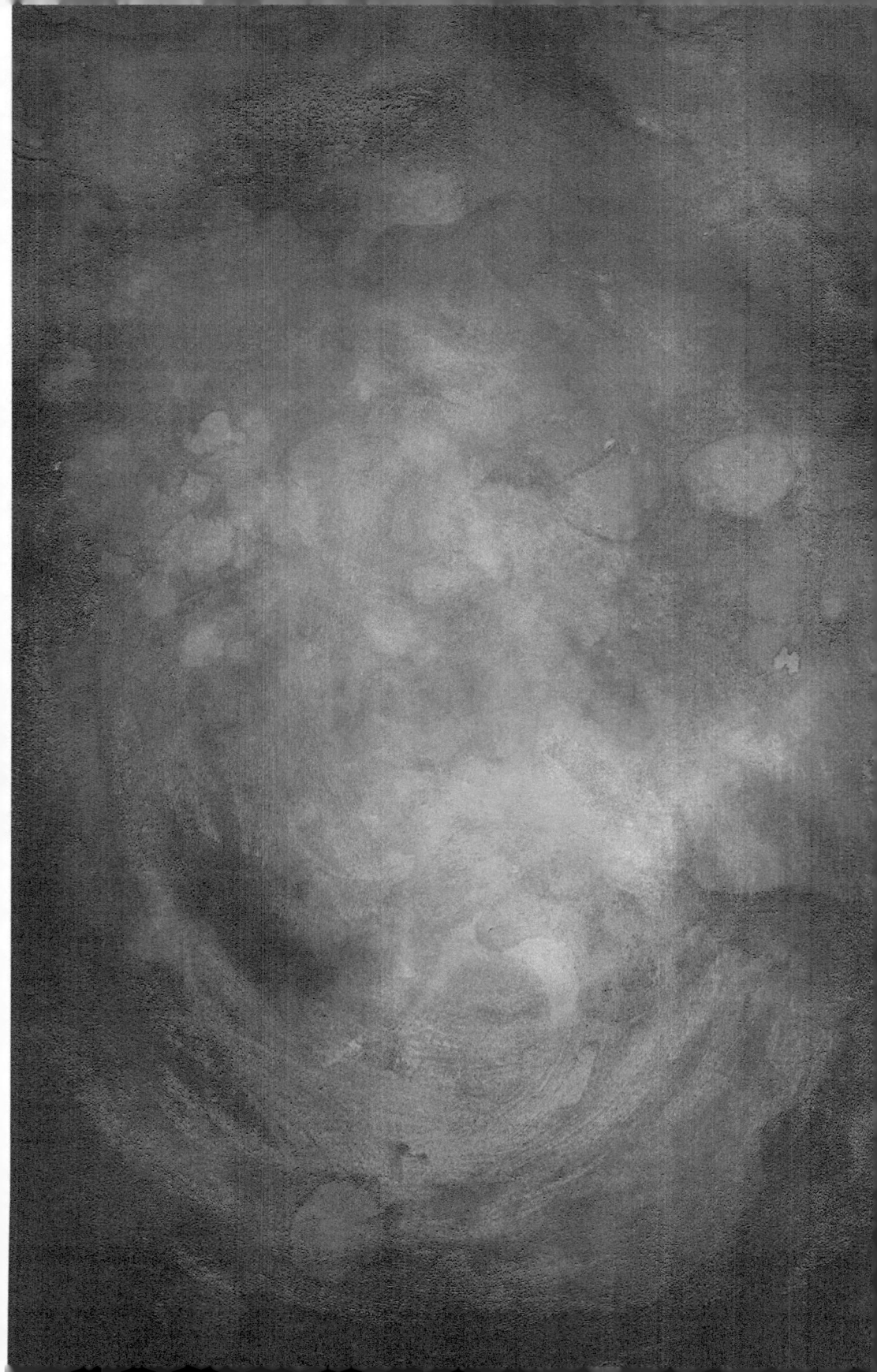

LOST IN MEMORY

Variations of Love ©2025 by **Lost in Memory**

Cover Design: **Hannah Luck**

ISBN: **978-1-964912-00-4** (ebook)

ISBN: **978-1-964912-01-1** (paperback)

ISBN: **978-1-964912-02-8** (hardcover)

Variations of Love

Divine

I find it hard to tell you
Difficult, if it gives you a better grasp of my hesitancy
I'm petrified you'll figure out my weakness I hid from the curious
You… you scare me
Terrify
Your beauty is unmistakable
Your heart is gold
But your soul is far from what I ever hold
No, divine
I! Can't! Lie!
As paradise manifests before my eyes
You… you were somebody that was unattainable, but yet so close
And I'm afraid
Afraid this paradise is an illusion and you're miles away
That… that this is all in my head
And you are what I always dreamt in my bed
Gentle touch, as chills remind me
Reality could only make me feel like this, and I put all doubt behind me
But it doesn't exempt me from all my fears
You are still somebody I could never be near, but you're here
Telling me
There isn't a place you would rather be than next to me

Past

Moments you asked me to relive
Moments you begged me to forgive
Moments you didn't want me to wallow in
You turned your head away
Stared at the sky, you and everybody frozen in place
And the moment came, when grass grew faster than the tear forming at the
corner of your eye
I asked, "Why are you crying?"
And the seconds you didn't reply the more I tried
But time no longer abides by our lives
And you tried to hide what's been torturing you inside, but never could I
It will continue to stay
And this is my mistake
I became blind
Forgetting why I remained by your side
The truth was better as a lie
And I stand by you the same way I found you
Confused about what the world will bring
But with me, before I made it a thing, you saw it differently
Because you believed I wasn't like everybody
I left something behind today
Watched your face stay in place
Wiped your tears away
I kissed you on the lips and took a knee
So that when time finally ease
I'll be the first thing you see
When our past is no longer hindering we
I'll say it and it will be
The last time you'll hear it from me

Angel

I want to, but I know it's frail
Tantalizing
Mesmerizing
Your soul
Beautiful but torn
And I crave to repair the tears and sores
You're hard to ignore
The world has been harsher to you than lives before
I want to protect you, nurture and reward
You're an angel
Fallen and worn
You're beautiful
Appearance and more
I want to
But I can't be more
I want to
But I must ignore
The angel and my hopes for more

Caged

If you promise, I'll promise, I'll hold you close
And truly believe you aren't just here to silence what's killing me the most
I'll play along
While you kindly rip it off
Because I'm tired, tired of feeling this ache
No matter how long I've neglected it, it finds a way
To resurface
To remind me of the chase
But to be honest, I want it to go away
And once you would reveal what cause me so much pain
Without hesitation, my foot would kick away
Attack until I made sure that I would never feel this pain
To put fear into thoughts
Second-guess the temptation to fall
To let it know it's wrong
But…
It's my fault
Instead of accepting your aid
I keep trying to run away
Instead of healing this pain
I'm begging you to put out the flames
You are what keeps me safe
From hurting what is pulsating underneath my rib cage

Smile

I couldn't stop smiling today
Saw her face, couldn't turn my focus away
She made my day
Unaware, as I gaze
Appreciating every expression, she makes
When she smiles, I quake
She has a spell over me, there's no mistake
She's everything I seek, and she's right here in front of me
An angel
A queen
The reason I smile and believe
Perfection isn't a farfetched dream

Forbidden Love

I ain't keeping no secret
Your love is my true weakness
Even if angels turn their wings away, you are the only angel I appreciate
The world's view is evil
But my love for you is beautiful
If we have to find another way, to express our love to each other in a public
place
I'll still kiss you the same way
We wouldn't have to accommodate to the demands of their wicked ways
Because our love is more than what they say
They could label us with what they may
No matter how hard they want us to fix our ways
Forbidden love is what they'll say
But our love is as beautiful as the people who condemn our ways

Cycle

As you yell, spewing fire at me
Screaming, as you do
This home
It's broken
This love
It's frozen
This moment
Your face is in pain
Hopeless
This notion
Tears
Sob
As I saw
The expression when the notion has veered off
Regret
Misery
Heartbreak
Anxiety
It's inside of me
Dying as you are crying
Debating
But now we're fighting
Oblivious to the fact, memories are imprinted in this shack
Is it worth fighting?
"Stop lying to me!
Tell me the truth.
Before you undo everything, we worked towards to."
Words are simple to speak
Actions are the words you keep
It's what you'd told me
Words I took lightly
It didn't define me, and now you are crying
Trying to decide if we could ever be
Denying this will always be me

Lying to make yourself feel guilty
Siding with the negativity
Loving the bad parts
Trying to have a heart
No longer is it a crime
Only a mistake that will be absolved until the next time

Fireworks

Signal flares
Fireworks shared
We are here staring at the sky filled with colors in the air
The things we did, made us understand what is
Cupid's pair
Googly eyes, stare
Time expired to act on impulse
This time, missed opportunities won't fall through the gaps of hope
The heat of the moment had reached its pinnacle
Two different souls collide and formed love at its inception
We joined hands and listened to our beating hearts and wishes
Impulse decision
We slowed dance and finished what we began with
A moment under the fireworks
No longer are we finding words
Only that time hurts
This moment that stops earth

Your Healing Medicine

I know it's selfish to say, but I want you to be the reason the sickness goes
away
Remedies could cure all the pain
But your kisses replace the anguish I endured, like a Band-Aid
No matter how many tablespoons I need to take, nothing is better than the
words you say
It sounds ridiculous
But a doctor can't take away what your comfort could
It's stupid to say
Your healing powers save me from the plague
But it's more than you think
Because I want to be treated like I'm worth healing
It's silly to say
But your love can do more than what modern medicine provides today
It's selfish to say
I enjoy these days
Because I know your love will be the reason, I feel better that day

Sobriety

It's a day we speak of
A day that can only be made in fairy tales or fantasies
I wipe the blood from your lips because I feel guilty about what I did
Altercations
Fabrications
It's not pretty
But when we lay and speak of things that patch these injuries
Beaches and verses keep those problems from furthering
It just doesn't stop the hurting
But we chose this life, filled it with lies until our thresholds create a new line
Like the roaring sound of a calm sea
Rough terrain, but it doesn't seem
Until the waves come crashing down and we are sucked into the possibility of
drowning under the sea
But it always seems it's never meant to be because we always see the beaches
of our dreams
Even if it is us being washed ashore
We can still be grateful for another chance to adore
Because eventually, we won't need to sing to keep us from drifting back into
our horror
But until that time, materials of our faults form underneath our eyes
Needles and bottles
Just a few reminders of why
We sit on our thrones watching silhouettes act out what will happen if we
continue on this road
Tears fall by the wayside and the waves finally drowned them alive
We closed our eyes
Holding each other tight because we knew it will be a matter of time
I look into your eyes
Because between you and I
It's easy to hide
To escape to this place
To tell our lies
But I have as well as you, used up all our time

Gave love to a drug and told ourselves no one else could love us because no
one else could understand us
But we hindered our growth
Gave evil its jolt
These things we speak of
These beaches we think up
Are only for us to run away from
Figments that we are part of
But do you get it?
Why you mean so much to me
It's because you are all that I see
You accept me for who I am, even though you know the issues that I have
Because you're not too far off too
But it doesn't mean we can't make ourselves beautiful
Improve what the drugs have altered
Allow ourselves to live where things can't falter
Because reality is all I dream of
To have you by my side is all I need to get by
But I know it won't change overnight
Because one day I will hold you and worry if your eyes will connect with
mines
The simplest things we lost touch of
Numb the nerves, and we are less of
But I hope you can comprehend
To fail gives you another chance
So, take my hand
Because all I know this could be our last chance
To understand reality
To finally meet who we are… in sobriety

Wildfire

Twirling in the meadow
Fire incinerates
As we dance in the blaze
We ignited a flame that we couldn't contain
Setting the world ablaze
We flourished until the rain came
Extinguishing the flame, we thought, was more than a spontaneous exchange

Smut

I want to show you who wears the pants
Grab your hands
I want to kiss you from your neck to your back
Bend you forward and slap your ass
Dig in
I want to lick both ends
Spread cheeks
Insert every inch
Feel every ridge
Arching back
Swapping spit
Reach around
Rubbing clit
Thrusting
Clapping cheeks
Biting skin
Press
Massaging tongues
Firmly grip
Constricting
Rolling back
Smack
Offset the constant attack
Smash
Until it drips from your crack
Put it back
Until you could say
You never had it like that

One Last Dance

As the day fades, light hides, and the night becomes our new torch in the sky
Stars reside at the surface of the dark blue sea
Water at a standstill
Time escapes
Air evaporates
My heart accelerates
I'm afraid
My hands shake
My body aches
And I can't take the daily reminder that you're still here in a place where I
could escape
I caress your face
Hoping your skin still feels the same
Even if angels exist in a different space
I could only hope heaven will let me save the only touch I can't duplicate
And you hate I can't move past what used to be
But how could you blame me?
When you were all that I need
But I understand what you mean
Because these eyes
These tears that fall from my sight have already cried too many times
And hoping sooner rather than later we will reunite
Fills your heart with the same emptiness life left me with
So I will oblige
Just grab my hand
Hold me tight
And dance with me… one last time

Words into Actions

You intimidate because the sorrow reached deep
That the sorrow became a living being
You grab my hand and pulled it close
Telling me you'll take the pain away if I let you console
Spoke with words that sent waves through my soul
I cling on to them with every fiber of my being and hope… your words won't
lose their tone
But you ensure it won't
By promising me the actions that will solidify words that you've spoke

Wish Upon a Star

Darkness
Moonlight
Twinkle, twinkle
As stars sparkle
Showering
You and I
Watch stars funnel into your eyes
You told me when it's over I didn't have to wish another night
Because this time you'll be what I have wished for all night
I look at the sky
Noticed the sacrifice
Gazed into your eyes and saw what I've been wishing for all my life

Accuse

And here you go again, accusing me of not caring anymore
You insist
You knew
Somehow you could read minds and drew a conclusion to
A conversation we had
Words that I apparently said
But that's you
Manipulating words that are not true

Forever and Ever

Flowers bloom
My heart goes boom
As we play under the moon
We won't go home tonight
Until the moon falls to the wayside of this lullaby
And here we go
Speaking
Taking
Asking
Wondering where this all lies
We scream love will never die
As stars and clouds watch us tonight
But please believe it will come to light
Even if we have to fight
But that's another time
As the moon hides
And the sun gives us life
It starts all over again
Speaking, acting upon this love again
As we treasure and hope, we can have the pleasure of loving each other
Forever and ever

In My Eyes

What the world defines as beautiful
Distorted, because through my eyes when you're in sight I can't look away
You're beyond the world's consensus
Because I don't agree with their assessment
I could lie
Stare at what society tells me to like
But you're the reason why my heart feels high
In my eyes, you're one of a kind
And why beautiful is no longer defined by what they like

Unlovable

I'm beyond repair
I get that
Or far from saving
I've accepted that
But…
Could you make an exception?
It's selfish to ask
Because it's not how it's supposed to work
I understand even if it's fake
The joys I could experience wouldn't feel like a mistake
It's a big ask
And unfair to expect you would be okay with that
But I just want a chance
To understand why our hearts need that connection
It's difficult for me to ask
Because I know what you see
And better yet, I have a better understanding of me
I know it's mean
To be selfish and hope you surrender to my needs
How disgusting it will be
To be with someone unlovable
To suppress unwanted feelings
Something I know you won't have to ask from me
Apologies won't rid you of those memories
If you dare take the risk with me
You'll have to live with that mistake for eternity
While this deviant gets to experience a special feeling
When love is given and received differently

Your Dirty Little Secret

I'll hide when it's convenient
Keep lies to protect your interests
But when I have you to myself
Where you could feel comfortable being yourself
I'll forget all that pent-up resentment to hold you close
Because you feel good to my soul
The absence of eyes
I find reasons that should be fine
When we are confined by a paycheck, wasting precious time
I keep you on my mind
When we lock eyes, and it's the only way I could express how much I want to
say more than hi
It kills me every time
I admire you from a distance and watch you exist
You're so lovely, and I wish I could walk up, and this barrier didn't create this
rift
And when you catch me, you see the joy in my face
Instead of the pain behind the pupil, you can't resist when we are in our safe
place
You never say it because you make it up when we are alone
And I never question it because I already know
I don't want to ruin it… because I hope

Music

The rhythm
You couldn't hang
The flow spoke to you at a different wave
It showed
The beat you were dancing to, not in tune
We were out of sync
Listening to different lyrics
Singing
But when the music stopped playing
We heard each other clearly
Leaning into each other
Beginning
Conversations
Different stimulations
And we tried it again
But as the music played
We knew the music didn't play the same

Sense of Duty

It becomes complicated
As time loses its place
We found distance, that made the situation tougher to explain
Planes fly over our heads while the earth shakes
Accepting my fate because the story leads where it needs to be
And you hate every second that it breathes
Because every sentence didn't have me
And I could see
The struggle in your eyes to keep the pain inside
I couldn't do anything to stop it in time
But hold your face and wipe the tears you cried
Promise you a future that could be broken with a blink of an eye
And tell you how much you mean to me
I embrace the pain that fills you inside
Because I know it might be the last time
I want to hold you
Keep you by my side
But I wouldn't be able to
If planes continue to cover our skies

The Game

With a smirk unbalancing this charming face
You knew I write tragedies for my own gain
To lie with many women who were tricked into the game
You have the audacity to believe you could change this dog's ways?
I play for the pleasure while you take chances for whatever
It's not my place to tell you how to fall into love
But you know there are dogs who seek for other pleasures that don't involve
love?
Be mad that you were that easy
But don't be upset that I got to do what pleases me
Because honestly babe, it's you who chooses to believe
Tragedies that are written in movies replicate my life so perfectly
But I'll let you off easy
Call me when you have the urge to be with a man who doesn't give a damn
And I'll accommodate you
Give you a little tickle when you feel in the mood
Because, babe, all you need to know
Is I got you

Shame

I was to blame
I made you feel ashamed
I came along and filled your heart with what is wrong
Gave you an idea on how you should be
I made you feel equal to me
I did this, so you didn't leave
That you were at arm's reach
I slept comfortably through the nights
As you fought with words that riddled your mind
I know what I said devoured you inside
But as long as I was happy, I didn't mind
Now you're broken inside
Fighting demons you didn't need to fight
I can't take back the words that define... your beautiful side

Red Ribbon

Marked with the red ribbon
Shallow seas
And the promises you made with me
The moon dwindles
While the sun swivels
We could play with each other's hearts, as long as time lets me
Complete the endings we didn't see
Find broken parts that broke from the pressure of the heat
I made dreams sprinkle from afar
Only heaven can speak what we could only see
And we are complete
Lovers apart
Marked with the red ribbon that bonds us in my sleep
The one who was stolen from me
Red ribbon
The token I keep
To remember you when I sleep

Afraid

If I could say what I really wanted to say
Would you be okay with the man I am today?
I'm not okay
I've never been
But you fulfill the emptiness that's deep within
There's this face
Different from your name
But a face that resembles what I've craved
Love easily replaced
Your name easily erased by another who could solve this dilemma I create
You stop at a distance
Side eye
I understand why
But let me explain
I can't remedy what I can't change
Because I've sealed truths from eyes and woven threads of lies
Fabricated reality from mines
Illustrated a realm that doesn't define what has been eating away
Because I chose to conceal the pain
By making sure you could never have a place… to settle in my brain

Young Pups

As it was told in books
Fairy tales and other tall tales
Love was the word tossed around young pups
In this transition of hope to find love at one stroke
We lock lips on the prayer that sparks will flourish deeper than ever
We held hands to enchant
To long last
With words filled with truth in the sky
Lies were only told when each other told one another that they could stay up all
night
Swinging our feet at the surface of the deep blue sea
Seeing stars fall from afar
We wished many of things
But the one thing we didn't seek was the love we only believed to be
And it was easy
Falling in love with each other was the simplest thing
Understanding why people couldn't see our love lasting for eternity was
baffling
It may be the beginning
But we will overcome all the little things
To prove love could be contained by the naïve

Issues

Knowing you have issues
You're not defenseless
Light enriches them and you become more defensive
It's hard to believe you have depression
Because when we fight, you take advantage of your condition
You do these things that make me question
Even though it may seem
You contradict yourself with every action
But I know what it feeds
So, I play along with the distractions
Excuses for me
But I know when it happens
I'm able to be
The better person and leave

The Fourth Dimension

In pitch darkness, I feel your hands press against my cheeks
Pucker lips, I feel you
Not physically but spiritually
And before you could plant your kiss
The darkness that consumes, vacuums
No longer am I consumed by the countless stories I've written about you
But a blank canvas you spoke into existence
Ripples, footsteps fade with each step
You breathe in another dimension I can't comprehend
But I feel you somehow, someway
Speaking to me on a different wavelength
And when I try to be where you want me, in a different plane
Resistance reverberates
And I can't bypass the fabric that keeps us away
But when your hands caress my face
And you look deep into my soul
I lean in for a kiss, searching where we could coexist
But I'm still unable to feel your lips
You melt in my arms
And we are back where we began
In the darkness where I was lost in

Heaven's Bell

If I could speak freely
I'll whisper it into your ear
I want to be relentless
That you are sensitive
That just the tip of it
Euphoria will be endless
I want you to know
Every time heaven's gate opens
I'm there ringing heaven's bell
Worshipping every second
Deviant
I want the hand of God to place pressure at the back of my head
So, there isn't any separation from heaven and hell
Just the ringing of heaven's bell
Until the bell can't take the ringing from hell

Broken Hearts on the Floor

As grenades fly
Streaking across the sky
I see them land in front of me, exploding into thousands of small pieces as I die
I cry as life escapes me
But respawn because laws don't affect me
I go into the furnace again and fight with her by my side
Watch rain turn into wine
But as war always does
No longer could this soldier accept proxies running around for fun
The only motivation to keep me running around this matrix
Were her words that told me to keep moving
To keep pushing
But as she continued to tell me this, I wondered what it feels like to die
Why?
Because pain nullifies when it's constantly inflicted a thousand times
And I wanted to know how it feels to die for the last time
To want what happens next to be real and not a lie
So, I walk in front of grenades
To see if I could get a taste of the void that consumes when reality whisks us
away
I reach and wait
To see for once if fantasy and reality could amalgamate

I Don't Say it Enough

I know it hurts
But as I saw you deal with it through the years
Time hasn't been the nicest part of life
With a tear running along the love, that is undoubtedly true
I know there isn't much time for us to appreciate this space we have taken for
granted
But words have to be said if actions were never received as intended
My heart, deep and plentiful
You filled fully with the love that is unconditional
And I know those words were never expressed as often as it should have been
But it was always received by our connection
The longing for your existence other than the memories we've created
The reason to inhale the air and appreciate it
Enjoy the fact there is a face behind the love that keeps me sane
You bring the best out of me when I would rather have accepted the mundane
It's hard to tell you
When it should be the easiest words to say
But it's what makes it even more meaningful when I say your significance to
my success
Not my fortune, but my livelihood
And you've enriched my days because of your existence
Even when my days seem darker than they really were
You were always the light that brightens those dark days
And I know it will always be late
Because it could never be said often enough
...
I love you

Obsession

I blame you for the simplest things you do
I found myself loving everything about you
People told me I was a fool
But I believed that when I fell, you would be there to catch me
But you didn't come through
I begged
I cried
That I forgot why
Why I continued to follow you when you didn't care when I tried
But I continued to have faith
Continued to believe you'll love me the same way
Obsession was the stigma you left on my plate
When you kiss me on the forehead and told me you were going your separate
way
I wanted more than the simplest bye
I wanted it all, even if it meant my life
I begged, and I cried
I told you, I can't live without you in my life
Hoping that'll change your mind
But you thought it was a lie
So...
I wrote a letter that told you why
Explaining to you what was so hard for you to see with your own two eyes
How much your love meant to me
How far I am willing to keep
The only person who makes me complete

Dance

Your arms sway in the silence as havoc ensues
Your mistakes thrive in the spotlight, and the emotion you're lost in gives
motion to your moves, and the deeper you'll go into your moods
I feel your pain
The problems you have, the escape you are trying to make
I have the same
But I express it differently
But it's all the same
I'll move when you move
And probably then we could dance in place
To the chaos that is crumbling onto us today

Love Lessons

I only turned you away when I knew you wouldn't need me
From the beginning, I assumed an everlasting
Took in all the baggage you carried
Even the secrets you said you would bury
I accepted you for all your mistakes
Even when you weren't happy with the decisions you've made
That wasn't my place
If anything, I made sure I showed you how to handle that pain
Not only that, but how not to step back in your old ways
Love was never in question
But how I treated our relationship made it feel like a lesson
I kept searching for teachable moments instead of existing in the present
Which became apparent
I couldn't love you the way you wanted me too

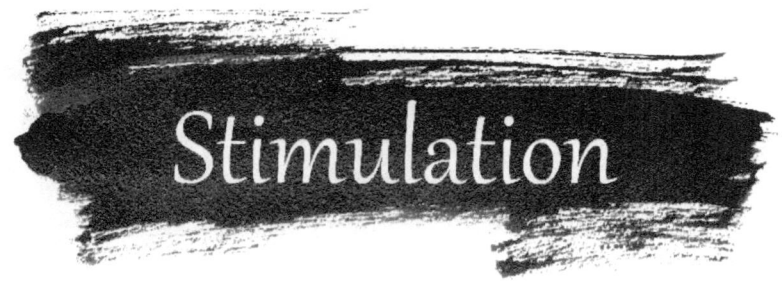

Stimulation

I wanted you
And it became so obvious that I did what was needed to be with you
But the one thing I won't admit
The reason we are at a distance
I'm afraid I could no longer stimulate a part of you that kept you interested
And it's not fair
That I'm so concerned that I will no longer satisfy you, that I keep that
important detail from you
We carry a label that keeps us aware
And it creates rifts unwarranted but clear
If it continues to go on like this, our hearts will bear
The resentment from my indecisions and fears
And you try to ensure me, "Your heart is safe with mines."
But I told myself a trillion lies
To know life could be derailed by one truth of mines
Unfortunately, I can't trust the person who I think is the love of my life
Sorry won't do
Because I'm breaking your heart every time, I tell you
Excuses you've become numb to
And when I lose you
It will be too late to tell you
Why I felt I couldn't do
The things I did to satisfy you

Use Me for the Night

Use me for the night, it's all right
I knew my heart was on the line
For the time being, I kept a good lie
But I didn't say it wasn't a fight
I tried, but at times, I put myself in a hole I kept digging myself in
But that's my fault
I understood why, and I know you did too
Because I shared some of my deepest secrets with you
I hated every moment I talked to you because I knew I would love how your
voice soothes
My greatest nightmare came true
That was falling in love with you
Painful because I was nowhere near you
But what made it even more difficult
You preferred it that way
Because you didn't feel the same
There wasn't much for me to do but get lost in the nightmare I become
accustomed too
I left my heart out at the window
Hoping you'd grab it one day
And I'd be able to see your pretty eyes and face
I wish I didn't think that way
But every time I talked to you, I couldn't control what my heart would do
Because every day my heart built a home for you
Hoping you'd come through
But I knew I wouldn't be opening the door to you
I tried not to think too deep about it
Or create fantasies around it
But there was nothing I could do
I was deeply in love with you
But you knew
So, when I say use me for the night
It's because I always wanted to feel how it would be like
To have someone listening on the other side

Lost in the Rain

The rain poured heavily on us that day
You stood there in a gaze
Lost in your safe place
I watched you
I craved
I understood you made mistakes
Some unforgiving
Some you kept hidden away
I couldn't say the same
But the way you made me feel
I was lost in the rain
I embraced the emotions you gave
I caved
Fell into your love
Asked for something I couldn't get enough of
I placed my finger against your lips
Telling you to keep your secrets
And as the rain continued to pour
My heart ignored
Your open sores

Gift

My head resting on your lap
If there's a way, I could never forget the gift you gave
I'll take it all to the grave
The love you take
Impure, but you accept it anyway
And I can't explain
How much I appreciate the sacrifices you made
I'll live to repay
Until my dying day
You'll know no other way

Ammunition

Sparks of light disappear as soon as they appeared
I captured your face in that split second
Did you feel it?
When the room went dark, and we bled out
The vulnerability
Because right there and then
You had every bit of me as I had with you
Gun loaded
Standoff
Forget what had happened
When smoke left the barrel, eyes shook
And we couldn't disarm ourselves
The trigger was already pulled
We acted on impulse
Because it was easier to put pressure where it hurt the most
Instead of dealing with the issue like common folks
Blood splattered all over the tile floor
And there was no way of cleaning the stain
Exclaim
That was the day
We killed the love we made

Chance

I watched the rain fall
Turning away, the best of us
I swallow my pride
Thought twice and asked if I could stay the night
Empty inside
I saw the reason
But I still need to know why
Was it a lie?
Or a man who told you he would hold you through these nights?
The reason I ask
It's because I want a chance
A chance that I know has been compromised by the many men who hurt you
inside
I'm willing to show you
How far I'm willing to console you
Give you more than I am asked to
Because I only want the best for you
I understand men have made you rethink the meaning of love
I understand I stand in front of you as one too
But please take the chance on me
Like I'm willing with you

Water of Bliss

As her lips touches mines, I immediately fall into the water of bliss
Engulfing me in full, luring the boy, who screamed, "Love has died slowly
inside this silhouette!"
Bubbles surface as I sink deeper
Light shines as it becomes bleaker
Her hands reach out for the seeker
Daytime dreamer
Pulling me in deeper
Neither could I find
Oxygen keeps me alive
But she's doing fine, and I couldn't understand why
How come I'm affected, but she still thrives?
Which I decide the sun is where I should reside
Because everything doesn't seem right
Time has a place where I fight, and I rise
Land is where I repeat
Searching for love, where I think it should be
But it's a funny thing
I keep looking at the sea
Which I finally see
It's where I should be

Hourglass

Will you love me when we have nothing more to hide?
When the sand drops its last bits on the other side
Will you still have the will to turn it on the other side?
When every sentence that could be constructed has been said a thousand times
Will every word still feel like a butterfly flapping inside?
Mortality became a different promising of life
Eagerness to see what happens when we die
Only because the sand bleeds into the other side
We spoke to each other when we knew it was almost time
With tears falling
Your wrinkles aged with mines
If there were more, I would still choose to die
I couldn't ask for more than what you have already given me in this life
Therefore, I'll wait for you when your soul reaches mines

Sweet Dark Melody

Chilling sounds of grief tremble down your bones
Whispers of the ignored one who wished their words had a home
Fingertips clench on the back who chooses to stay
Who listens to the mockingbird that plays the same tune every day
And you lay your head on his fragile shoulder, that has too much weight to take
on your mistakes or another
But he lets you lay
Singing sweet dark melodies in a tender way
Sending chills down his spine that urged him to run and hide, but denied those
urgencies to keep you up right
Until he lied
His shoulder became dust
The man who stood untouched became bothered by the evils you were
accustomed of
He was afraid of you
He lied, not knowing what he was getting himself into
You fall to your knees
Curled into a ball
Wept until you fell asleep
But was awakened from your dream by a melody you've sing
You open your eyes and to your surprise, it was the man who left you behind
He sings your song and tells you he knows what he did was wrong
And asked if he could fix your song that had been haunting you for far too long

Pretty Letters

I tried to make it sweet so you can feel every word that I speak
Pretty letters so you can read
Telling you things, like how beautiful you are to me
Or better yet, it's you and me under a tree with a pleasant breeze holding hands,
as it should be
Pretty letters so you can read
When your mind is on me, thinking about the little things, like a baby giggling
on a swing
It's nice
It's sweet
Pretty letters so you can read
The little things we sing
La, la, love in the spring
But it's hard to sing when we read pretty letters from me
Pretty letters so you can read
What you loved about me

 Apocalyptic Weather

I walked outside hoping to catch a glimpse of the world ending
But what I saw is my life beginning
From the bursting of the stars, I did not see what it was all for
Until it crashed down on me, like a falling asteroid
It only left an impact on what I should look forward for
I said it would feel nice to die by the hands of my own instead of time or from
another man
I let the worst part of my emotions tell me it was okay to think like this
I used it as my happiness
To watch one another
To understand, we will always be together
You made things a little brighter under this apocalyptic weather
I kiss you under the acid rain that fell on us to kill the pain away
I understood for the first time how to feel alive because you helped me
experience that for the very first time
So, when the rain burns our sorrow away and I look at you as somebody who I
would give night and day
I smile because I get to love you everyday

Beauty and the Beast

Nothing could do more than her presence next to me
I am no more than what I depict myself to be
A monster amongst the living
An evil to the people that walk along this evil
She stands close to me
And I found refuge in the beauty of her complexion, the silence of her
perfection
I couldn't help this fall
I found the marvel of them all
The moment she closed her eyes, she showed vulnerability
She told me without saying anything
"I am no longer the idol you put me up to be.
I have my scars like any regular human being.
This complexion, this perfection, is only skin-deep.
I found pain in the same realms that you let yourself be.
I am an ugly human being."
No longer is she bothered by her dream
I flip her hair back and see
What makes her so beautiful… is because she's just like me

Leap

I'm scared
Brown eyes
Fear
When I stare and you're there
My world crumbles at my feet
And I'm not sure if it's healthy to think
That once I step
There could no longer be you and me
You plead
Begged for me
Timid
I'm afraid if I make the leap
You'll realize, and I'll fall into obscurity
It doesn't seem we're meant to be
Insecurities
You tried to ease my mind
But the devil is knocking and I have to answer
"Why?"
You don't deserve what I put you through
But I still want you by my side
Selfishness
But you're okay with it
And I know it's not right
But inside I'm fine
As long as I have you waiting for me
To never do what is right

Personal Servant

Soft-spoken
Sweet
But I'll grab your hair and give it to you until you scream
I'm just a man who fantasizes how it would be like to be between your thighs
Having you breathing heavy
Giving you the power as you look and wonder
How could an innocent tongue be fluent in cunnilingus?
As if I skipped a meal
A buffet is open 24/7
And if you let me, I'm taking residency here
I want to be your tool
Your gateway to ecstasy
Your sexual servant
The catalyst to explore your deepest fantasies
Have your legs shake
Wondering where is the earthquake
Pound the cake
Until the batter is dripping off the plate
Lick away
I want to live between your legs
Make you feel a certain way
Sensitive
Because my tongue has been there all day
I want to give you that sensation everyday
The one you call when you need that relief
Even if that's all you'll need from me
A personal servant to fulfill your need

Beauty

Washed ashore
Hair damped
You're more than I could ever imagine
I try to tell myself to breathe
To catch a second wind
A moment to think
Your beauty
Breathtaking
And I couldn't be any more undeserving
But you speak to me as if I'm every bit as worthy
Hard to believe
But it's the reason I journey
Across the seas
To witness what could possibly be
Limitless
You've given me
No reason to search when you're all that could be

Hierarchy

From the heart, I raised my glass high and locked eyes with hers
As I toast this glass to the King and Queen, I hated the fact that I couldn't be
her man
Which in return I tried to hide who I am, to fit the ideal man
It killed me
"King and Queen, I'm a peasant of the East."
They told me after I spilled everything, I was foolish if I believed the princess
could love somebody who they spit on in the streets
I didn't want to believe
But confounded by her stance, the princess agreed
It didn't end there
She continued until I concede
Harsh but true
Our hierarchy keeps this love from flourishing
Something we already knew
-

Late-night excursion
Holding hands
Marrying
Sweet nothings
Ogling
But the specter of being seen looms heavily
Because this escapade could be what sunders this endless dream
And before we could expect it, the King's guard found her and I
They dragged me away as she watched and cried
Taking away the opportunity for me to say my last goodbye
Imprisoning me for loving the love of my life
-

Water drips
This dungeon deafening
Sanity on the brink
This prison eroding me
But the starlight seeps through the aperture where my heart wishes and dreams
for the princess who dared to love me

But these brick walls keep that from happening
Tattered robe and a scarf to disguise
A peculiar individual decides to grab my attention from what keeps me alive
Unveiling before my eyes, to my surprise, the love of my life
She and I kiss of what was missed
And when she and I could rip ourselves from our lips, she professed
"Ol' dear peasant, where can we be?
To love for eternity with no hierarchy to adhere to.
Ol' dear peasant, my love and only king.
I will break you free from these walls of evil deeds.
Run away and form castles without worrying, what restricted you and me.
Ol' dear king, take my hand and promise me.
That you will always love me... even after everything."

Moonlight

Water creeps between toes
Footprints washed by the shore
Ashes of the past came too early to cast one mind to look back
And I found myself hating myself even more
I can't cope with what I ignored
Not anymore
I saw you
In the ocean smiling like you used to
I'm sorry
I'm meek
If you still remember me
Say something
So, I can believe
That's all I need
More than you ever seek
You are special to me
I dive in, into the ocean where you loved to be
I knew you were telling me, silently
I just couldn't see
The burdens you held
The emptiness you felt
I was too busy with me
But now I want to be
Where you always wanted me

Something on the Side

I run my fingers along your body
Begging for more than a kiss
What we do in the dark is our secret
I promise you, even from afar, my lips are sealed
Like how I feel
We tell ourselves only for today
But we know tomorrow comes and the week plays
We crave each other each day
But there's a secret I keep to myself
A secret I'm afraid to admit to your face
Sex is a perfect disguise
And you'll only see it like that until I can't hold back why
Which is why I fuck you as hard as I can
To have you entertain these thoughts that I have
But I'm afraid the only reason you have stayed
Is because of the orgasms I gave
So, I don't say what I need to say
Just appreciate your body before you go on your merry way

Meadow of Yarrow

Do you remember?
The meadow covered in yarrow
What we saw before our eyes
Changed what we thought, what life was
The laughter
The joy on your face
Running as our hands glide above the meadow, we embraced
No care of what will take place
I could feel your heartbeat
The calmness you emanate
You plucked away
Smelling the perfume, the yarrow generates
And your eyes open
And what you saw
If I could be lost in a moment
It would be here with you
Because as I turned to see what astound
I knew
This meadow of yarrow would be a place we go to
When things were simpler… for me and you

Colors

A splash of paint
The colors I bleed when I am with you
Are the colors you mixed when you knew
These colors mixed perfectly with you
And you see
The rainbow wasn't all it could be
We
Knew
The endless amounts of possibilities
And we seek
A color unique to you and me

Endless

From a distance, you see the water exhale and inhale
As you stare, gazingly
The fear of not knowing
As the tail of an asteroid bleeds a purple hue
The forsaken
"We've been here."
As I held her hand
"It never gets normal.
But we deal with what happens next."
The only way to reassure her everything will fall into place
I hold her tight
And close my eyes

-

The soil entrapping my hands
The weight of my body, heavy
The absence of strength
No will to turn and fight, accepting my fate
Ready for the steel to insert and catapult me to the other side
But the clinging of blades making contact energized
Adrenaline high
I turn to her
My knight
Her blade dances like a wave
Re-wrapping the hilt
As I remember the day
On the sandy beach waiting for the waves
"Do you think it was a mistake?" she said
Not knowing what to say
She replies with another sentence to keep my mind occupied
"Maybe it's easier to believe in one absolute instead of many."
The heathen's blade ran across her chest
As life escapes her eyes, a smile releases the pain buried inside
Rage
And I swung my blade

Overpowering him until he could no longer resist my pain
I run to her side
Trying to tell her before I meet her on the other side
"I don't."
Crying as I hold her in my arms
"As long as I am with you, I'm willing to see it through."

Commit

How could I find peace when there is somebody out there better than me?
Love is cheap, diluted by society
Insecurities have already ruined me
Giving more ammunition to what I already believed
I don't want to be yours because it's easier to walk away and not feel like I
could be replaced
That's a scary feeling
It's not you, it's me
My unwillingness to commit to somebody who could find better than me

An Angel's Touch

When I look into your eyes, I hope angels are as forgivable as you
Hazel
Blue
I'm not the man your father would approve
Broken and confused
I've isolated myself from what is good
So, when I see you
I understand your complexity can't be defined by your beauty
And deciphering you is something I haven't learned to do
These tales were visible to you
And you saw this devil that stood before you
Fractured
Abused
A simple touch would shatter the truth
So as gentle as an angel's touch
You've found safe havens where you could reside
Without shattering the dens where evil hides
Finding paradise in unhabitable places
Whispering lies to convince me I was wrong all this time
I try not to
Hold on to
Hope
But with you
I want to
You know
Subtle gestures
You spot
Holes
And you approach
Cautiously
Hoping I won't close
Tricking the brain
Unconsciously
You try not to fold

Just so you could hold
Something I hold close
But I know
Because I won't show
Something that doesn't need to be consoled
Anticipating this day
Pulled from underneath you
I'm to blame
I can't keep leading you this way
Because I crave what you crave
Out of kindness
I'll protect you from this tragic space
Because you should chase
Somebody who pulls you away
From where I choose to stay

Symptoms: Blindness

Would you understand the precautions I would take
I just don't want to scare you away
Because I understand clearly
The perception of me
Or at least it's what the world told me
And I know timid hands can't console what your heart yearns for
I'm just not sure if you're aware of what you are getting yourself in for
Because blindness is a symptom that develops when it's this close
I just don't want to hold you close and cure the disease that gives me hope
I just hope you know
Even though you say you're willing to take the risk that nobody was willing to
take
It's okay if you decide you made a mistake
I won't hold it against you because you didn't know
And that's my fault for not telling you
Because I was being selfish without thinking about you
I already feel guilty for what I coerced you into
By showing you the pitiful side of me
I'm not proud of what I did, but it brought me closer to
What I hope could be true
And I know it's not fair to take your valuable time in exchange for mine
And I know sorry won't do
The repayment is steep that I know will be hard to repay you
I can't commend you enough for the sacrifices you'll make
But I promise you for how long you are willing to take
I'll do what I can to make sure you don't feel like you've wasted the time you
gave

Brave & Afraid

Sun fall
Illumination
Night
There's nothing that you and I haven't already seen
Stars rise
Eyes dazzle, but our reflection escapes
Reluctancy
Unwillingness to let this dream breathe
Space
Distance
We
Ask ourselves internally
Is the risk worth the pain
Ripples underneath
I yelled for you to stay
Leverage gained
One foot forward
You weren't trying to flee
Weak
But you saw it differently
Meek
You didn't use it against me
The silence, deafening
Brave
Afraid
You and I are of the same
I did more than elaborate
I gave you context to why
You gave an ear to bear
A hand to conceal
We no longer fought this fear
If the heart is willing
Let it be here

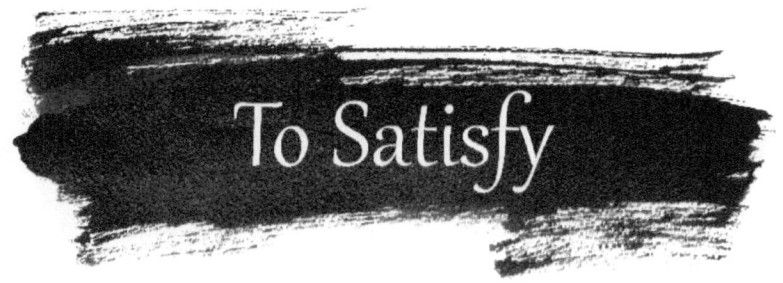

To Satisfy

I want to surrender power over to you
On my knees
Beneath
I want to make your legs feel weak
Feel them shiver every time my tongue licks between
I want to hear you breathe
When every flick from my tongue gets you closer to ecstasy
I want you to feel like a queen
That you should always expect this from me
I want you to sit on me
So, you know I'll do anything
To have your pussy suffocate me
I want to give time where you need
Sitting down as I please
With your legs out
And my head in between
As you press my head closer to show your dominance over me
I want to be your leech
That it's hard to keep me away from what I believe is the sweetest treat
I want you to bend over as I feast
As I lick from one end to the other
So, you know everything about you is everything a man would eat
I want you to know if that's all you need
Is me satisfying you until you're sensitive beneath
It will be
The stimulus I'll ever need

Talking to the Moon

If my words don't carry through space
And you're not sure if I'm thinking about you throughout the day
You could always listen to the rhythms of the moon when I'm wide awake
Trying to mend what's left of my mental state
Because the escape helps me cope with the pain
Don't place blame where I share all of it
Just listen carefully to the tunes you bring out of me
And know that I'm able to voice these glorious lines of affection because of
you
Even though it hurts me
I'm just happy I could say lovely words about you

North Star

"When the stars escape, you could always count on me to lead you the way."
Rain, as the night coated the streets
The umbrella you held with both hands through the evening
By the stop post
Intuition drew you closer to me
Like Rudolf, cigarette
Flick
As I was ready to pull for a taxi
Your hand stopped
A surge of memories rushed like a geyser
And...
A tear shed
I hug you tight and I never knew why I felt I was missing you all my life, but I
understood why
Kisses for days
And I ask if it was okay if we stayed a little longer
The smile that never fades
You nod your head, and we accepted our days

Sacrifice

Laughing and playing
Innocent but hurting
Do they see?
It's foolish to think they don't hear our screams
The idea of leaving
It's hard to fathom
Naïve
A reality fractured
Disaster
We protect them at the expense of our own
But would they understand why this can't go on
I don't know
Are we beholden to their happiness as we grow?
Or are we able to search for our own?
Cruel
And when we look at each other hoping we could recapture that moment
We knew salvation isn't in either me or you
Watching from the sliding door
We knew
Either decision will fuel
Their views

The Battle of Love

The blade bleeds
Wings flapping against wind
Each hand moving kinetically different until the blade released its grip
Scream
As he falls gracefully to his knees
The mortal catches himself from hugging defeat
The winged angel descends to his feet
Dragging the tip of the blade to finish the deed
The mortal bleeds while the angel musters the energy for one last heave
Raising the blade over his head
Battle worn the mortal fears imminent death
Hurling downward to release life from the burdens it kept
Contact
Disperse
Flowers were what felt the hurt
Split second
Surge
Rib cage
Dagger
A sweet release
Behind, the mortal holds the angel intimately
Resting his head on his shoulder lovingly
Disappearing from sight
From burning buildings to the starry night
Yarrow catches them and holds them tight
By each side
The mortal brushes the winged angel's hair away and tells him why it had to be
this way
"I only craved for your transcendence even in your descension.
Never did I ever expect this would happen.
But it happened."
Caressing the mortal's face before the sensation fades away
"I never wanted to hurt you."
Coated in pain that the winged angel contributed to, life escapes

"I just wanted to defy our truth."
Losing vision, sight
Nigh
"Even if it meant going against you."
Before the winged angel said its goodbye, he kissed the mortal a goodnight
"Your love is with mines until eternity finally decides… to sever ties."

A Swirl of Emotions

Lovely
Soothing hums
Body heat
Perfume
Smooth skin
Goosebumps
Breathing down your neck
Tears shed
Emotionally overwhelm
Rollercoaster
Your hand leads
Free-falling
Envelop
Bedsheets
Descending
The melody of your heart
Settles
You bite your lips
Dive
Lost in a swirl of emotions
Holding hands
Clashing waves
Whispering winds
Waterfall
Intoxicate
Spells
Time is just a construct
Thrill
Cripple
As the notes pluck away
Fading into ecstasy
Bathe
Swoon

Drifting away
Into the spirals of the milky way

A Streaking Star

As you run, a streaking star flies over our heads
Laughter and joy
Tears trickle
Reverting to our innocents because it's all we have until the void
There's no escaping this
Our fate has been given
But we could cherish this
A blinding light
As your face is filled with glee
A reminder, you were the reason I breathed

Regret

Before these tired eyes rest, forgive me
I've known about the decay that has been eroding away
There's no apology that could excuse why you didn't too
Regret
But my actions should have never been, if you meant as much as I said you
meant
I should have disclosed
I just felt you didn't need that placed on your soul
But who knows, maybe if I told
I wouldn't be here ready to rest my soul

Indulge

Echoes
Moans
Panting
You lose control
Closed eyes
High
Sensations
Lies
Biting lips
Zone
The more you ask for it
The more you know, the harder it will be to satisfy your soul
Indulge
Go
Your appetite grows
Exceeding your threshold
Loathe
Null
But it still gratifies the hole
Tormented but whole
Misery keeps a place to sleep
As you feed it with glee
Echoes
Moans
Panting
Indulge

The Skeleton of You

I unbury you because I'm afraid of letting go of who had my soul
Because with you I could relive moments I thought we would continue until we
got old
I could pretend somebody else could replace this feeling
I could find purpose in a different person
But I can't let you go
I know I'll die alone
But at least I could cope with the skeleton I used to hold close
And never know… a life without you

The Sandy Lagoon

You wiped away my tears
Running on the sandy lagoon
Laughing in the midnight blue
You broke me into my fear
Moonlight shined heavily onto you
I began to lose my faith
I realize things cannot be the same
You found ways to slither in deeper
The way you made me a believer
I love your lips
Your eyes
Your smile
And the wink you'll give me when you catch me staring
I can't live without you
Engraved hearts on the sandy lagoon
You drag a stick to lead me
Petals that are settled on the coastline
The moon leveled
Kicking feet
Sitting on the deck where you could see the clouds and the other finer things
And it couldn't be
Sitting by you is heavenly
Beneath the stars that are as beautiful as the sea
Shimmering equally
The wind draws us closer
And made it a little tougher to let go of each other
Resting your head on my shoulder was all I need to get over
And I cannot help, but to think this could be as powerful as wealth
You wiped away my tears
You wiped away my fear
You wiped away my faith
And most of all
You took my heart to a different place that it wasn't familiar with until today

My Fair Share

Rain
You see, I see
Pain
Cloudy skies
Hide
I've seen my fair share of troubled lovers, but you take the pie
I
Find it easy to push away
To preserve my sane
But I can't look away
I wouldn't want to live this way
It's why I could understand your pain
Because I've been there and felt the same
Your name won't be used in vain
I will remind you every day
What they have taken away

The Hardest Part

When she's gone
And pictures become too much to bear
How am I supposed to cope?
Because she's gone doesn't mean her ghost still doesn't roam
Or her voice doesn't echo
Even impressions are still visible
I can't let her go
The hardest part is you didn't take us both
And now I know how hard she did her best to null
I know what I'm about to ask is a sin
But you understand without her I can't function
I've given enough of my time to the people I love
Now give me back the time you've taken from

Doubt

As you exist, I'm caught in the moment
Do you feel the tension?
Telepathically
Peripheral vision, absent
But I'm here wondering when time erases the time it made, and then creates
Will my name still be brought up every second it accumulates?
I know this is just a phase, but doubt plagues
And I'm not sure if I could get out of my own way before time meets its day
I don't know what to say
I don't want to bring up an idea to shorten my stay
Neither do I want to stay silent when uncertainty has rotten my brain
Existing with you while time ticks away
Living with it because I'm afraid
That either way will sunder my hope you'll stay

Word Gymnastics

It's hard to explain the gymnastics that go through my brain
To find the words that could explain how each time you continue to amaze
Beautiful doesn't seem the same because you outgrow it each day
Perfection doesn't sound the same when you continue to redefine it in so many
ways
And it's hard to say, one day, it will find its way into my vernacular
But I love the chase
Because when that day comes, I will know what to say

Ecstasy

If I could, I would spend most of my time pleasuring you sexually
Worship every inch sensually
Ecstasy
Have you bent with my face dug in
Flicking until your legs give in
I want to catch you
Sitting
Watching
Enjoying your day
As I sneak up, entering intercourse to spice up your day
Have my fingers crawl from your chest to your most sensitive place
Rub it slow
Build up a flow
Until you are ready to explode
I want to watch you moan
See you squirm
Kiss your neck to your chest
Nibble your nipple
Sensations
I want to make you have it all
While we are still clothed, I want to fight with fabric
As you have contractions
I want your legs to lock tight
Constricting my hand as I try to get you past cloud nine
While demonstrating my might
I want to be between your thighs
Giving attention to the nerves that have you moan my name
I want to feel your legs wrap around me as I eat away
I want to hear you breathe, in a way that has me believing you ran a marathon
today
I want to lick away the juices you exude from my relentlessness to pursue your
flower to fully bloom
And I want you to understand this to be true

That I want to do everything I can to appease you
Because you deserve to feel beautiful

Beyond Belief

You're beyond belief
Perfection doesn't come close to what radiates before me
I can't believe you don't see what I see
Angel from above
Flood gates open
Heaven doesn't know what it has done
Words are hard to find
Because there's not a word that could define
What heaven left behind

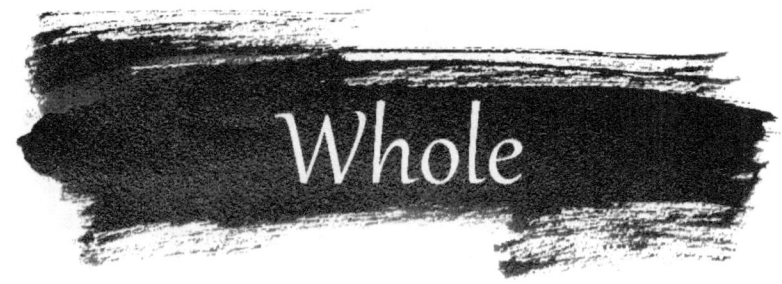

Whole

As the blood trickles, your arms cradle my heart and soul
You see life as we know it
As I see the merging of the two
You're in my ear whispering I love you's
Glossing over
Projecting
The darkness layering my pupils, plays movies
I'm still here listening to you
I don't know what to do
Afraid of what is true
But you, I hope, follow through
A world unknown
The possibilities grow
But never showed what's behind its veil
But here
With you
A bittersweet moment
Because I have a few seconds to cherish your existence
Numb
Your kisses are the only thing that is coming through
But before I go, I'll reassure you
To never lose hope
Because before you know
We will be back when we were whole

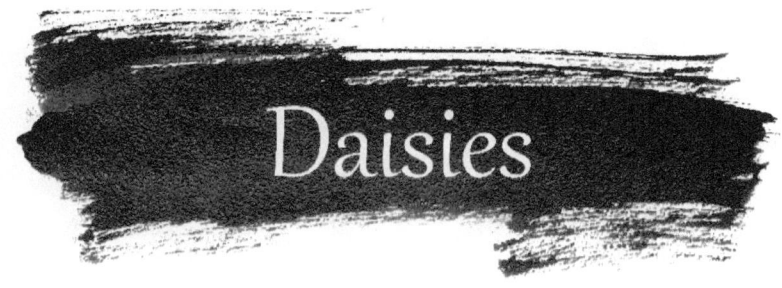

Daisies

On my knees
Two moons
Purple hue
I look back to see you
Walking away
Like rain
Stars fall
Display
Stubbornness digs my grave
But I couldn't continue to see you walk away
I scream your name in the hope it'll stop you from continuing the path you take
I take each step with adding pace
Full sprint, I grab your wrist to stop you, to explain
You pull your hand away
It didn't stop me from apologizing for my mistakes
You turn violently to tell me to get away
Frozen in place
As she walks away
Vanishing from this space
Daisies remove themselves from their stems and evaporate into space
Bare
Waste
My heart accelerates
My eyes focus on the brilliant display of light shooting across the sky
Lost in between space and time
Shackled by vines
Chest opens wide
And the beating stops but glows light
Petrified
Water falls from the only source of sight
Capsulize
Until daisies sprout from all sides
Immortalize
Until she realizes why

Bubble Gum

Bubble gum you pop with your tongue
Has that sexual tension built up enough?
If so, could we skip past the fluff?
Bubble gum
Cherry blossom
We could have some fun
Don't think twice, let's start the night, and not question why
Bubble gum you pop with your tongue
Pink watermelon layered with yum
Entangled tongues
We ran to hide, to explore each other's wild side
Sweat and cum
We exchanged love for lust and secrets with how we fuck
Bubble gum
We exhaust ourselves to a slump
Under the sheets, we felt each other's body heat and heartbeats
Resonating lost feelings, but that wasn't enough
To make this night perfect, I asked for more than what you have given up
Hesitant but willing
I did the same, and we were both glaring
Because what got us caught staring
Was realizing how unhealthy we were, on how we think
Love was just a word we exchanged for what we thought we need
Which explains both sides and how we are so willing
Bubble gum you chew intensely
Because now I see, like you see, the reasons for our cravings

Behind Every Good Man

I know what is wrong and nothing about that is right
I speak to you because I want to try
It hurts because I look at myself and know what stands in front of you
I can't change that
And before you ask all that is in the past
I can't rehash what I did and hope your perception of me will change
That's a scar that could never go away
What you see is someone who needs somebody to tell me that's okay
That you'll love me either way
I can't tell you the many ways I've learned to hurt myself without using
physical pain
When I see you I see a happier me
A person I've learned to love because you showed me, that's okay
When I stare at you
I see the architect that'll build what I couldn't
I'm not deserving of your time
What you see before your eyes is a waste of it
Selfishly
I'll make it worth it if you stay
And I'll promise you what you built, you could take it to the grave

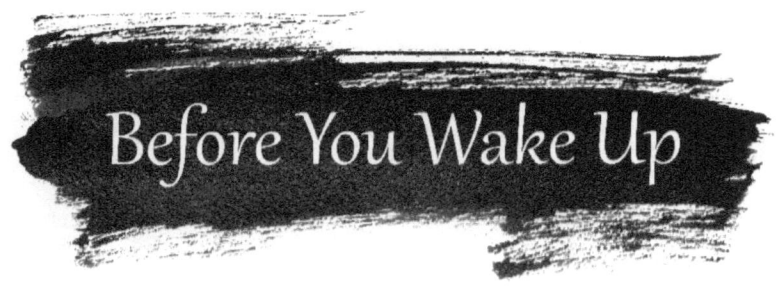

Before You Wake Up

In bed by your side
Admiring the space you take
Combing your hair trying not to wake
I'm ashamed
You deserve better, but admitting that to your face you'd defend me in every
way
There's so much I could say
But it would be unfair to you when you love me this way
I count the days
Knowing when you finally wake
You'll see your mistake

Blue Pearl

Fixed
Circling
Scowl
You soften my frown
Because no longer does the world seem like it's upside down
North
South
Hemisphere
I no longer veer
Because I want to be trapped in your atmosphere
And make it clear
I want to breathe your air

Needle in a Haystack

As you stare into the stars, I know deep down inside you found peace with your
decision
But that wasn't the hard part
As the world spins at the tip of your finger, you look at me
Smiling with tears, and said, "Memories. No matter what, we will always have
memories."
Wobbling
Her eyes closed
Spinning into the abyss
I chase as you weep in pain
In space, time is relative, and I can't remember the last time I've kept track
Needle in a haystack
I'm still floating to find the world we've created
Mapped out the stars to see where I deviated
And still haven't found that ounce of hope you'll join me to find the blue
marble we've molded
Plexiglass
My face imprinted as I searched every inch
But I know better and the risk I need to take
Suited up and faced the darkness alone
With a tether to keep me close
Cold
Grasping for anything that could give me hope
But as I float
The more I know
The deeper I go
The harder it will be to come back home
But the quicker it will be for me to show her, I found what made her let go
I cut the string and let the abyss devour me
Why, repeats through my brain
Like many other questions, I needed answers to
I made mistakes
I've done things I know that caused the axis to tilt out of place
But you never told me to not chase

Because you hoped that tether would keep me safe
But I drift with my oxygen tank
Knowing if I didn't find that world, we've built
There wasn't a reason to come back to an earth that's filled with memories
you've killed
With every inhale
CO_2
I've kept thinking to myself
If I found that marble, we've built
Would you comeback and help?

...

..

.

Bright light
Heaven's gate opens, and I know I can't change the decision I've made, but
embrace
Blurry eyes
And a silhouette tries to wake
Clear sight
And an angel greets me at the gate

Honeycomb

I love the way you moan
How my tongue circles around your honeycomb
Humming
Vibrations
You felt the sensations
I crave for your validation
I made sure there was no separation
My fingers added to the stimulation
Orgasmic ejaculation
Honey drips
And I lick every bit of it

Mushroom Clouds

We sit in the meadow, like children
Drunken by fear
Giggles
Suppressing, despair
Sweet nothings, but in tears
Kissing as a mushroom blooms
Eyes shut tight
"I love you."

Willing

The coward in me
I shrink in your presence
And with the little courage I have, I stand in front of you broken
Ready to shatter at any moment
Unworthy
Truth
I admit, I no longer want to be alone
It's true
I need help, and that's hard for me to ask from you
I will no longer lie to myself or ignore my heart
But accept what I've been running from
That is, you
And I'll surrender
If it's what I have to do
To prove I'm willing to learn from you
I'll stay up all night and all day
To have a better understanding of how to love you everyday

A Billion Simulations

Fingers dance with fireflies
Eyes follow
Rowing under a bridge
Ripples of the moon and stars
You're everything I wished
A sun didn't have to be sacrificed or plummet from the sky
This evening under your gaze
I offer my hand
You reach without hesitation and take this dance
On the pond with an audience
I'm not much of a dancer
I just want to keep your interest
To place myself in uncomfortable predicaments
So, you don't get bored with repeating my name over and over again
I whisper sweet nothings because I know your reaction
Playful beginnings
But you're a woman
Beautiful and sexy
I should acknowledge you, as such
Slow dance
But the audience wants more
So, I back that shit up and bump my trunk against yours
Embarrassing, but if I have you laughing on the floor
I don't care who's watching, I'll be your dork
Because if I'm not trying my hardest to impress you every day
Why am I wasting your time when someone could show how much you should
be appreciated?
And when you want to get serious, know my ears are always open
And I'll listen to every word you have to say
So, you don't have to bottle it all up inside and pop off when the fizzle exceeds
what the bottle could contain inside
Communication
I want to be open
So, there isn't a secret you haven't read up on yet

Arms dangling toward the pond floor
Fingers snapping
My eyes focusing on you like an iron sight
I'll pull you close
Eskimo kisses
Arms wrapped around every curve that defines your womanhood
Because you should be admired for not only your beauty but your sex appeal
So, there isn't a day you shouldn't feel you're underappreciated
I want to be your slave
Like, Spears or Tatum
I'll do whatever you want me to do if it gives me your attention
Know that even when I want to fill your days with smiles and laughs
Admiration and lust
I could always take your hand and have your head rest on my shoulder when
you want the pace to be slower
Listen to your concerns or worries
Or just listen without a word spoken from me
I could be flexible
I could give you space
You don't even have to hear from me the whole day
Because I don't want to be the reason you push me away
I'm afraid to lose your comfort
Or the space you've taken
I know it's backwards
But I just wouldn't want to go back when things felt the same
When you weren't an equation, I try to figure out every day
Which is why you needed to see this space
Where my thoughts run through billions of simulations of when I might see the
day
To make sure I don't lose you from my mistakes

Remedy to Cure

You were lost, and I found you
In the things you stood by… that hurt you inside
I'm hurting too
But I'm here to rescue you from the rain that pours inside
Heaven knows that you've cried
Umbrella opens wide
While the storm continues to try to hide… you
And I try to comfort your pain
To heal what's left of your heart
Which I know was wounded from the start
And in your pain, I tried to think
What words could be said, without resurfacing memories that are hard for you
to relive
Afraid that you'll push away
Lock the chain and throw the key away
I'll ask you to whisper it into my ear
And I'll promise you I won't tell anybody your remedy to cure
Just let me try to make you happy
Bring you back to reality
Better than what you became accustom of
So, you could find your way back to where you could love
Because I know I found that in you
Even when it eluded me
I saw it in you
And it may be hard to believe
Before we met in this horrific scene
Without you, I was everything society told me
Only with you, I felt differently
You are my everything
You're my one and only
You're that special one that saved me from myself and everybody else
I was lost, and you found me

The Dock

I sat at the edge of the shore wondering where these footprints headed toward
I could see it lead to a dock where romance found its war
Battlegrounds formed
Love and hate took their place and formed a new definition, and it begins like this:
"For every lover that brings you great pain. Leave them and search for another that doesn't do the same. Don't rest even if they are the opposite of what you think. Watch for trends and once they revealed themselves again, say goodbye and never again."
The bitterness this dock brings shows love in a different meaning
As hate mutates into a different being
There is no more separating mixed feelings
Imprinted into thin air
Their whispers echo into my ears
Laughter came after and the naïve played out their disaster
Ghostly figures side by side
Holding hands with feet kicking in sequence in another time
She leans in for a kiss, pecking him on the lips
He asks for more to fill him
She gives in
Loving him loving her in sequence
They disappear
Walking on the shore laughing even more
Lying on the dock, pointing at the stars in sprawl
She lies on his chest, feeling his heartbeat
The reason for love changing so quickly
Death by a loved one who she loved immensely
She blamed her lover for everything, while he tried to find her reasoning
She told him why, and he didn't understand why he was to blame for his life
She said she would have been able to say goodbye if love didn't occupy time
Pointing fingers in the wrong direction, that led to things that shouldn't have been present
Love became different when both lovers knew it was time to create distance
They instead sat at the edge of the dock waiting for the other to be the reason

Causing hatred
Not comprehending stubbornness is settling
And their decision would cause friction
But it didn't make any difference
They couldn't see past their existence
They held hands on the dock where they found love
They kissed on the ledge, smiling before they dove in
Only understanding, the next time they'll see each other will be better than this
life they were given
Because they believed things would be perfect the next time they would fall in
love again
And I sat on the ledge looking at the sky
Seeing them finally okay with their demise
As they reach for paradise
I lie on the dock where I will meet mine
Hoping I don't follow behind lovers who discovered hatred for each other

Bleeding Pigments

Like a rose, delicate as it could be
You have thorns to protect yourself from me
Anger represents how the pigments bleeds
Hostility, your distrust in me
Like a rose, delicate as it could be
Hatred, you've learned from me

Nurture Back to Health

With arms cross
Hair covering your face
Is it selfish to say?
I waited for this day
Because when your mind is correct
You'd be wiser to stay away
But I have you wounded
Easy prey
And I hope, when I take advantage of you in your most vulnerable state
You could understand why I feel okay brushing your hair away
Untucking your arms as I reach for your chest where misery drains
"I know the feeling."
As I hold her heart
"But I don't know what you're experiencing."
Caressing it with my hand
Head down, ashamed
"I want to take this opportunity while I can.
To uplift you where you can stand.
And see you be the best you can."
I reach
Pulling a spoiled beet
"It's not much, but as long as you know, I'm willing.
It will be a substitute for somebody more deserving.
Just let me remind you why you are so worthy.
Before you lose sight of your beauty."

Revisiting the Well

When it drops
The heart skips a beat, and you wish you heard it differently
But it's never the case, it's always the same
I hate the fact that you want me to play like that and expect it to be all right,
just like that
I wish it were that easy
But doing something that sleazy
Wouldn't be fair to the person who treated me differently
I love you, and that's a fact
But you can't understand why I can't come back

Porcelain Tub

Submerged in a tub of water
I sink my head into the tears I shed and saw the heinous acts I committed
Placed blame on the love I said I would only cherish
If only I meant it
My intentions were never in her best interests
I fought for every period in every sentence
Used every excuse to make her look wicked
I never said the things I should have said
Only reminders that kept her from lifting her head
When I look back at everything we did
She was the reason it made sense
But she will never know it because pride did more than kept things I should
have said
It kept her from pursuing passions that would surpass anything I did
And it begins
All those repressed memories I kept hidden within
Resurface with the bubbles that escaped lips
I just hope if we meet again
My newfound love could heal what I've did

Honey Dip

Let me lay you down
Lazy fucking
Sideways
Dry humping
Kiss your neck and back
Firm grip
Rubbing your nip
As I have a hold of your tit
I want you to beg for it
As my head teases the honey dip
Pleading for my hand to rub your clit
The smoothness of your skin
I don't want to go unappreciated
Because that would be a sin
To not appreciate what God had taken his time with
As you turn for my lips
Locked eyes
I know you're hurting for it
No need to say it under your breath
I could feel it on the cloth you wet
I place my finger on your clit
Slowly rubbing it
Lubrication
My fingers are wet from digging into the honey dip
Drip
Temptation
I want to lick the jar clean
But you want my focus to be right here between teeth
Heavy
Heaving
I didn't change the pace
No need to chase when I'll get you there, anyway
Squirming
As it starts to be hard to contain the honey from overflowing from the jar, I've

tasted
You beg me to continue to rub you that way
To keep pace
As you fight from pulling away
I could feel your heart race
As you are about to ejaculate
I continue to kiss away
As your legs shake
The honey escapes

Rain of Fire

Ashes fall
He's in awe
He turns his head
"Burn it all!"
Yanked into darkness
Paralyze
A growl overpowers
Shaking air
Its presence, almighty
With the will to jolt his head to the sky
Bright red eyes look down
A gush of wind blows his hair wild
Ruby-red eyes descend to his line of sight
Its breathing became his
He dare look the devil in the eyes
She walks by its side
Grazing its rigid skin
Until her eyes match his
Her hand out
Catching ashes
"You came to conquer, but you're left with a sword in hand and a wooden
shield.
What you didn't account for is the inevitable."
Blowing the ashes off of her hand as the wind whisks it away
With each step, she made toward him
Ashes ascend and dissipate
Elongated nail placed underneath his chin
Petrify
Face to face
She says, "Gods and angels fell from the sky. Demons cowardly hid further into
the pits of hell. And who are you?"
The ground shakes with each step the beast takes
Casting a shadow
Nostrils flaring

"An appetite that is bottomless; tell me different."
Sword and shield fell
He holds her gaze in fear of speaking, but his eyes told her, "Help me."
Its mouth widens
Vacuums
He didn't let go of her gaze
Within its bowels, fire conjured up but held its place because she is what ignites
the flame
"Fear crumbles the weak. And you'll become susceptible to your worst
demons. Fear conforms ideologies."
With both fingers, she lowers his eyelids and whispers
"To willingly fear is to tell a different tale. Your willingness to fear is to
blindside the threat. To attack."
Whispering back
"Or get as close as I can."
He opens his eyes, and she's stunned
He replied, "To fear is to show the threat, vulnerabilities, so that it could be
easy to find theirs."
Grabbing her hand, placing it on his chest
Her brows slant and her nose flare
Her eyes burn red
She yells, "Incinerate!"
He pulls her close as they were being poured with a rain of fire
"To fear reminds you of what you should hold close and not forget why it's
important to you."
When the beast realizes it was burning its queen, its burst of rage stopped
With its teeth
It rips him away, and she falls to her knees
But it wasn't done with him
Ready to rip him to shreds, she halts it before it can
She crawls to his side
Nearly to a crisp, he says, "To fear is to prevent, what if?"
She grabs his hand
"To not look back and wonder if I would do it again, or let the mystery stay
hidden within? Be content with what has happened because at least I won't
question if I left it as is. There won't be a reason to revisit it because I made the
decision. Even when I was mistaken."
She kisses him on the lips as his ashes ascend
She holds onto what he said
Knowing what he meant
And promises herself when someone like him comes along again
She'll leave her dragon in the dungeon to give him
The opportunity she didn't give to the rest of the men

Space and Time

Fill me with happiness
Fill me with lies
Tell me everything is going to be all right
Dance with me under the lights
As space is underneath and stars are our surrounding
Tell me this will last until the end of time
Kiss me until our tongues tie
Send me your heart so I know it's mine
Look into my eyes
And let's fall in love every time

Cold War

Fireflies bright up the night
Illuminating, demonstrating with their light
Rising from the pond, we held each other tight
Kissing one another like if it's our last time
Whispering words
We hoped
We lied
Telling each other, "Our love will last until we die."
The only uncertainty we have in this life, but time had something else in mind
This scenery of tranquility became a place of misery
And we looked at each other differently
Which brought us close and forced unwanted feelings
We told ourselves fibs just in case we could rekindle what time did, but battles
were being set for what was up ahead
We swore if it ever came to that, our love would be what stops it in its tracks
Never did we think war could be fought differently
Silence and words that cut deep
We forgave each other, but lingering thoughts we loathed and sheltered fueled
our animosity for the other
The only thing that kept us from letting it fester
Were the recycled memories we treasured
It's what kept this bond, but didn't mend what was wrong
The hand kept ticking on as new life spawned
Thinking that will fix what was wrong
It delayed the battles that were already waging on
Which we realized what has been going on
War never changes
Only the battlefield and the way we wage it

Touch Me

I want you to touch me
Not sexually but intimately
Fill my heart with feelings
Remedy the disease spreading within me
Touch me and help me break free from the ugly things that haunt me
Touch me to give me meaning
Touch me where only you could reach
Touch me because you love me
Because your touch is all I need to feel something

The Tale of the No Heart Fiend

I wonder, is this how I die
Writing endlessly into the night
I closed my eyes
Trees surround
Birds chirping
Sun setting
You lift the cover
And you read the story of a man with no heart
How he walked with a scowl and let the village people know, he's to be feared
He went about his day
Isolated by his ways
They learned his name
And the stories that were told
The menace
The monster
He was the evil he spoke of
As you turn each page, you've learned why he was so feared
But yet you were naïve
You had to believe nobody was born this way
This book explains why this was the case
And the last page brought you to the woods where he stands frozen by his rage
A statue, blackened by his pain
Green scenery
Pleasant feelings
And this statue feels out of place
There had to be a mistake
Trepidation
Even though your heart is in the right place, you tremble in fear
As you see, the man who brought so much terror
But you had to see for yourself
If what they speak is what you should believe
At his feet
You see, the scowl they spoke of
The anger that radiates from the statue

It became hard to breathe
Because of his presence
You feel the tension building
Part of you wants to run and forget you ever saw the man you read about
But the worst part of you; told you to do something people warn you of
You place your hand where he had no heart
To see if maybe if you could feel a resemblance of one
But nothing
Unease, you felt pity
You look up and stare at this man
Unsure what to think
You turn your back and walked away, but as soon as you did
You hear the statue crumble
You turn to see
As you witness your undoing
The man breathes heavy
Slowly, the anger in him melts the coal that encapsulated this unforgivable soul
That scowl is no longer frozen, but intensified as he sees you
You realized
Run and hide
As he chases you through the forest
You could feel him breathing down your neck
As his menacing growls for blood stiffens your joints
Fear paralyzes
As air becomes scarce
You feel his presence behind you, but you dare not look
But it didn't take long for your lungs to surrender
You collapsed and hear tree branches and leaves crunch
You closed your eyes
Hoping for a swift death
You felt his hand reach for your throat
Clasp
Legs flailing
As he raises you from the grass
Trying to release his grip
Oxygen thin
You see, the fire in his eyes
You understand now why
In your last attempt to see more time
Your hand hits his chest
And you felt his grip loosen
A gift
You punch, and he tightens his grip
Figuring it's his weakness
But as you barely have the will to clench your fist

You place it firmly against his breast
Nearly blacking out, you drop gasping for air
As he squirms in pain, catching air
You see, a man in fear
You're in control as he lays defenseless on the floor
Scared of the one who towers over him
You wanted to do what no one could
You raise your hand, ready to strike
As you see him ready to fight
You would have given him the power
As you realize
Your scowl was like his
You soften your stance
Quieting the anger built inside your heart and kneeled
His eyes widen
Feral
He's ready to snap
Your well-being wanted to back away, out of fear you won't escape if he
grabbed hold of you again
Your hand slowly creeps toward him
He, ready to flee
But before he could
Your hand grabs his ankle
Paralyzing him
You look into his eyes as anger no longer is in sight
There was fear
And you were prominently the fixture of his gaze
The glossy figure encapsulated in his maze
No matter how badly he wanted to run away
You had him in your spell
No matter what will
He was frozen in place
"Let me go," he says
You forgot this man had a voice
"Let me go!"
You said ever so gently, "No."
He begs, but nothing was removing your hand from what kept you safe
"Let me be, and I'll promise you, you won't ever see me."
But you know in your heart once you did, he will try to do everything in his
will to make sure you never live
As your hand moves from his legs
He screams frantically for help
To belt
His pleads for help became more enriching
Abdominal

He yells
He's squirming, trying to escape
Like a dog cornered
He's in a frantic state
Part of you could feel his pain
The fear he is feeling
His threats thin
His words with no venom
He's doing everything he can to stop you from what you never planned
Your hand
Lays firmly on his chest where they said had no heart
You felt it beating rapidly
Him screaming in pain
Screaming at you
Telling you the harm, he will do
But your hand is firmly placed
And his face didn't look the same
Hyperventilating
You slowly moved your face
Where he begs you not to place
You lay and felt his pain
The anguish
The hate
You listen as he begged away
Because that didn't explain what was going on underneath his cage
No matter how hard he tried to worm his way from your grasp
Your strength was overpowering
He became weak
Because your courage was everything he needed
You stayed listening
As he tried to tell you everything
You understood his words were full of lies, underneath is where the truth lies
Days became months and months became years
As you, both laid, as time withered you both away
You look at his face
And you see age
You didn't look at him the same
And when they speak their truths
They understand that's what they knew
Wiping the tear from his face
You kiss him and say
"I love you."
He kisses you goodbye, with the words he thought would have never been
learned in his life
Frozen in place

Stone
No one would know why
Lovers laid side by side

LOST IN MEMORY

www.ingramcontent.com/pod-product-compliance
Lightning Source LLC
Chambersburg PA
CBHW020412130626
46549CB00006B/2525